The End

Aditi Machado

THE END—and now what? Am I changed? Is the world? I've lifted myself off the page and what sort of gesture is this? It isn't especially dramatic, it happens simply, and I mark it. Poems do end, at least materially.

THE END: "You must change your life."

I must change my life!

I must read the poem and change my life.

Hah.

BUT *is* that the poem's end?[1] I re-read and now it says something like *you must, at all times, endlessly, change your life. You cannot* not *change your life.*

The poem is Rainer Maria Rilke's "Archaic Torso of Apollo" in the English translation by Stephen Mitchell. In it a grand sculpture of the Greek god Apollo stands before the eyes—grander, it would seem, and more ruinously beautiful for its lack of head, arms, and legs. "We cannot know," the poem begins. "We cannot know his legendary head / with eyes like ripening fruit."

That is to say, we begin not-knowing. The absent head confronts us and names us in our unknowing. How should we look upon this headless thing, "we" who have heads? The torso is so big, it is as though our heads are atilt, studying the empty space above the severed neck and chiseling into it the impossible eyes looking back at us.

> We cannot know his legendary head
> with eyes like ripening fruit. And yet his torso
> is still suffused with brilliance from inside,
> like a lamp, in which his gaze, now turned to low,
>
> gleams in all its power. ...

Compressed in Apollo's torso lie the features of his missing head. A gaze materializes in it; there is a smile in the musculature around the genitals, and everywhere radiant hair. Everything is getting magnified. The stone isn't

---

1 End as boundary in space and time, but also end as purpose.

simply gleaming, it's "burst[ing] like a star" "from all the borders of itself"—the torso is erupting out of its own material and the dim gaze that once was now gleams multiply out of multiple eyes: "there is no place / that does not see you." In the demotic, *you feel so seen*.

You must change your life.

"ARCHAIC TORSO OF APOLLO" is a sonnet. Rilke wrote it in 1908 while working for the sculptor Auguste Rodin. It is considered an ekphrastic of a fifth-century BCE sculpture called *Torso of a Youth from Miletus* presently located in the Louvre. Mitchell's translation of it is composed in loose iambics with enough consonance and assonance to say a sonnet-like pattern of end rhyme (ABAB CDCD EFE EFE) has been achieved: head/inside, torso/low, Otherwise/thighs, could/flared, defaced/fur/itself/life, shoulders/place.

Sonnets tend toward completion. Structurally, both the Petrarchan and Shakespearean forms whittle *down* (4-4-3-3 or 4-4-4-2) and synthesize *toward* a statement of some kind—the resolution of an argument. Thought arrives in tandem with the feeling of it having arrived. So it is with Rilke's sonnet. It is also the case that here the ostensibly complete form of the sonnet accommodates the incomplete—broken—body of Apollo which, in the process of its contemplation by "us"—by "you"—becomes complete. And then more than complete. So complete that it obliterates itself out of completion, returning "(y)our" gaze with an injunction of such intensity it eviscerates you and me, the human, the living, the changeable. The torso is not incomplete—*you* are incomplete. Your manners and perceptions, your knowing, the sense you have of your own life—all incomplete.

Rilke is no televangelist. He's more like a theologian of negation. In his poem the torso becomes legible as its awe-some self by way of repeated denials, deferrals, and negations that test our grappling with what is *not* coming to be known. In grammar every truth (there is no head) meets its counter-truth (there, a head). Grammar dangles before us the alternatives:

> gleams in all its power. <u>Otherwise</u>
> the curved breast <u>could not</u> dazzle you so, <u>nor could</u>
> a smile run through the placid hips and thighs
> to that dark center where procreation flared.
>
> <u>Otherwise</u> this stone would seem defaced
> beneath the translucent cascade of the shoulders
> and <u>would not</u> glisten like a wild beast's fur:
>
> <u>would not</u>, from all the borders of itself,
> burst like a star: for here there is <u>no place</u>
> that <u>does not</u> see you. You must change your life.

In addition, therefore, to the brilliantly radiating torso, grammar procures the torso that does *not* dazzle us, does *not* smile, appears defaced, remains unglistening, does *not* explode, and which maps the "no place" (utopia) that does *not* look at you so that you *don't* feel seen. Must you still change your life? I think so.

"EYES LIKE RIPENING FRUIT"; "THAT DARK PLACE WHERE PROCREATION FLARED": On the one hand, fullness, fertility, and excess. On the other, brokenness, barrenness, and nothing. You come to learn and what you learn is that something is wrong, something is missing. "You must change your life." Maybe you change it, then you come back to the poem and are told to change it again. Change is endless. The poem staggers on the cusp of knowing what it is to be complete while remaining incomplete. The end of the poem is there is no end. There is only the rest of time. The future.

Sometimes I think it means the final change: "You must change your life *into death.*" *Be like me*, counsels stone-dead Apollo with his graven posture and rampant, maggoty eyes.

THESE DAYS I write only long poems. To compose a ten-line poem, say, with a good first and a devastating last line—it doesn't move me. Though, of course, poems do have last lines and sometimes the last line devastates. But that's not (really) the (only) end of a poem. The poem's end is to endure.

I'll write the same poem for weeks or months at a time, composing almost every day at roughly the same time of day. It's like extending a single annotation over an obdurate duration.[2] I write to discover a form, but the form is also discovering the language and the thinking, and it happens out of order. (Lyn Hejinian in "The Rejection of Closure": "Form is not a fixture but an activity.") It is not decided in advance what the thinking will be, but inklings of sensuous and nonsensuous matters have been amassed in preparation. The system to writing is rhythm. Prosody prompts me to find ample instants of acuity to put together a structure in which thought and feeling can proceed/regress with and against the methods of time. Then I rewrite for one year or several years. I rewrite by hand and practice the shapes of the text as I reshape it. The phrase "No precision that isn't imprecision" haunts my practice. The whole thing drips with time.

---

2 A phrase I adapt from Rosmarie Waldrop's translation of Edmond Jabès's *The Book of Yukel*: "I am more obdurate than duration."

NEVERTHELESS, this essay reads almost exclusively short poems. Short poems emitting signals in smog toward some alien enterprise I claim as mine.

Longform practice wants to extend signals and "hazard improvisations."[3] It wants to answer calls from the crumbs of lyrics and rippling exteriors of institutions. It wants to think beyond its own time.

Paul Celan, translated by Michael Hamburger:

THREAD SUNS
above the grey-black wilderness.
A tree-
high thought
tunes in to light's pitch: there
are still songs to be sung on the other side
of mankind.

---

3 Deleuze and Guattari (tr. Massumi): "One launches forth, hazards an improvisation. But to improvise is to join with the World, or to meld with it."

NEVERTHELESS, there are short poems (imagine this were an actual taxonomy: short poems and long poems, and an arbitrary number of lines that arbitrates it: twelve? fifteen? seventy-one? I amuse myself) whose signals, if I can help it, I avoid.

Superficially, James Wright's "I have wasted my life" sounds not too different from Rilke's/Mitchell's "You must change your life," but actually it is different in almost every way. I used to teach this poem (from *The Branch Will Not Break*, published in 1963) when I first began teaching poetry writing courses. I think I taught it because it belonged to the unofficial anthology of teachable poems one inherits when one becomes a writing instructor. Also, I think I taught it because maybe then I liked it, or thought I did, and at the very least found it useful in its imitability:

Lying on a Blanket in Forest Park in Saint Louis, Missouri

Above, I see the orange hot air balloon
Half-asleep in the grey-blue sky,
Dawdling like a shadow the color of eaves.
Down by the ditch near the new prairie grasses,
Yogis follow one another
Into the distances of the …

If this[4] is too cruel, then may I at least point out that

---

4 The title of the poem is actually "Lying in a Hammock at William Duffy's Farm in Pine Island, Minnesota." The poem goes: "Over my head, I see the bronze butterfly, / Asleep on the black trunk, / Blowing like a leaf in green shadow. / Down the ravine behind the empty house, / The cowbells follow

Wright's poem arrives at its epiphany ("I have wasted my life") by means of a recognizable pattern[5] of experience as depicted in literature and cinema: the protagonist observes with increased intensity the things of the world, which provokes a realization that bears the contours of some profundity. There's a truthiness to "I have wasted my life" I can abide to the extent I abide a humanist concept of selfhood—which I don't. What's called "the speaker" of Wright's poem, his self-deprecation notwithstanding, is far too capable of naming and describing the nonhuman aspects of his environment ("the bronze butterfly," for example), far too assured of his ability to wield language-as-a-tool, to direct his own consciousness. There is too much of a zealous faith in perception (the "chicken hawk … looking for home," horseshit "[b]laz[ing] up into golden stones"[6]) absent an

---

one another / Into the distances of the afternoon. / To my right, / In a field of sunlight between two pines, / The droppings of last year's horses / Blaze up into golden stones. / I lean back, as the evening darkens and comes on. / A chicken hawk floats over, looking for home. / I have wasted my life."

5 I am hardly the first person to so characterize it. Rachel Zucker's "An Anatomy of the Long Poem" begins by quoting Jack Spicer ("generations of different poets in different countries [are] patiently telling the same story, writing the same poem") and goes on to articulate "description, bits of narrative, epiphany" as the prevalent model for the short poem. "Lying in a Hammock" is one of her two chief examples.

6 Whereas Rilke crumbles a dead monument into life, Wright monumentalizes a living present, turning it into a golden past. A butterfly lies still and bronze against a black tree trunk like a gilt frame on a museum wall. (I am aware, yes, of the existence of the species commonly called "bronze copper butterfly"; the association with art, for me, remains.) Sunlight is that other glitter, lacing the pastoral diorama with stupor. Even fertile

examination of how that perception[7] happens.

The scale of time against which Wright's poem issues its epiphany is the time of an Individual. The scale of time in Rilke's poem is the time of art and myth and human history. "I have wasted my life" is psychological, therapeutic. "You must change your life" is existential. It will not heal you.

---

dung gets to be dead gold.

7 Etel Adnan in *Of Cities and Women*: "Doesn't the act of looking at an object become also one of its definitions?"

I SEEM to have been discussing the short lyric as though it were necessarily composed of two parts: an epiphany at the end and the (mere) stuff (of setup) leading up to it. Rather, this is simply one pattern for the composition, which in itself is worth neither my favor nor my disfavor.

(There are poems that end on an epiphany that I like and those, like Wright's, that I don't. Yet I am not really so irked by this one poem as I am of its belonging to a sad proliferation of copies. And of what I believe is the role writing pedagogy plays as *agent suprême* in said proliferation.

I'm a pedagogue and I feel culpable.

There's me teaching, then there's the system in which I teach.

There's me trying to teach in new ways. There's me failing.

Here's me desperately not wanting to teach how to give good end.

Rachel Zucker writes that it is the "middle distance [that] interests" her and, you know, me too.)

But even the description of this pattern is troublesome, implying that the epiphany is somehow separable from the other stuff of the poem. A different conception: the epiphany, whatever that is, wherever it appears in the poem, is inextricable from the structures of unfolding out of which it emerges. The entire short poem, given to wrestling with the question about which it desires to be epiphanic, itself is epiphanic. I.e., the force that through the green fuse drives the flower *is* the flower.

THE EPIPHANY, WHATEVER THAT IS: An Incomplete Inventory:

- When I walk home from the bus stop, I sometimes have an epiphany about an event earlier in the day, how better to answer a student's question or how to fix my essay. A cartoon lightbulb floats above my head.
- Reality TV contestants not only have epiphanies but stylized formulae for delivering them in the filmed confessional.
- On social media, epiphanies arrive with the speed of self-help and in electronic bluster.
- In the oft cinematized narratives of personal success, epiphanies are stepping stones to self-actualization.
- In some Christian sects, Epiphany is a religious feast celebrating the manifestation of Christ as son of their god. It is the corporeal revelation of a theological truth.
- The Greek verb *epiphanein* means something like "to come suddenly into view."
- In modernist fiction, "the epiphany signifies a moment of clarity in which artistic or ontological truths are exposed," writes Maria-Daniella Dick.
- In contemporary United-Statesian poetry, epiphany is typically associated with closure or resolution at the end of a poem. In the preface to her critical essay "The Rejection of Closure," Lyn Hejinian offers as a "negative model" of closure the "coercive, epiphanic mode in some contemporary lyric poetry ... with its smug pretension to universality and its tendency to cast the poet as guardian to Truth."
- But if I remove from epiphany the expectation that

it offer closure, I begin to conceive of it, simply, as an aspect of the procedures of language. A kind of thickening up, a tendency toward music or noise, an opening out. In that moment, it feels like something is being made manifest—a corporeal revelation of some kind of (not capital T) truth. It's the "coming suddenly into view" of an elucidation. And as with coming into view of, say, a feature of the landscape when one is driving toward it, past it, ahead of it, one might move toward *and* away from the epiphany without it necessarily becoming the *fact* of the poem. The *thing* for which you remember it, if you remember it at all.

LET'S SAY that the epiphany is a moment of (re)cognition in language. And that it can be revised, or repeated, or forgotten.

Let's say that epiphanies happen in time, in noise, against surfaces, and "in" a range of subjectivities.

And let's say that Hejinian can be read as an epiphanic poet whose epiphanies do not foreclose meaning, a poet who dramatizes the *happening* of epiphany, of experience, in time and noise, against surfaces, etc. For example, Hejinian's chapbook-length poem *Happily* (2000) begins:

> Constantly I write this happily
> Hazards that hope may break open my lips
> What I feel is taking place, a large context, long yielding,
>   and to doubt it would be a crime against it
> I sense that in stating 'this is happening'

This poem keeps staging its own ongoingness. It describes many contexts.[8] The subject's philosophies proceed in those contexts, brushing up against its planes. Several pages later:

> Perhaps happiness is what we volunteer
> A cormorant appears in the sun flashing exact notes, a
>   phenomenon of a foggy day stretching its wings

---

8 Hejinian in "Some Notes toward a Poetics": "The context ... is the medium of our encounter, the ground of our becoming (i.e., happening to be) present at the same place at the same time."

> Madame Cézanne offers herself in homage with its various uses with its curve and blank stare
> It resembles an apple
> And the most unexpected aspect of this activity dependent on nothing personal is that it consists of praise coming by chance, viz., happiness, into the frame
> It is midday a sentence its context—history with a future

The same passage, with my reading of it in brackets:

> Perhaps happiness is what we volunteer [an idea being toyed with, an epiphany with an "if" to it]
> A cormorant appears [a scene/a context] in the sun flashing exact notes, a phenomenon of a foggy day stretching its wings
> Madame Cézanne offers [volunteers] herself in homage [to the cormorant, perhaps? or to the foggy day with its cormorant wings?—thereby she feels happy, I think; I hope] with its [homage's] various uses with its curve [note the curvaceousness of homage, for soon it becomes the curvaceousness of an apple] and blank stare [shine]
> It resembles an apple [the epiphany! the epiphany! the corporeal manifestation of an abstraction, "homage"; homage as an apple offered seductively to whom else but ME ME ME]
> And the most unexpected aspect of this activity dependent on nothing personal [not "me"; "not" me] is that it consists of praise [*laus*, that ancient, ever renewable mode] coming by chance [happenstance], viz., happiness [the poem makes an argument for happiness as a case of happenstance], into the frame ["a large context"; the portrait of Mme Cézanne]
> [The poem moves on:] It is midday a sentence its context—history with a future

Hejinian's epiphanies, when they happen, feel *spoken* in the course of thought. There's a chance-like quality to them. They happened to happen, were not inevitable, and don't contrive to achieve the feeling of inevitability; they're not virtuous. In re-readings of the same text, I often change my mind about where the epiphany comes or what it means or how it behaves.

By these standards, maybe Hejinian doesn't write epiphanies at all. Except I think she does.

Hejinian's poems never, in my experience, *end* on the epiphany. *Happily* closes with the experience of wind blowing against the body and the image, I guess, of it clearing out the space (the "large context") of the poem:

> No, happily I'm feeling the wind in its own right rather than
>   as of particular pertinence to us at a windy moment
> I hear its lines leaving in a rumor the silence of which is
>   to catch on quickly to arrange things in preparation for
>   what will come next
> That may be the thing and logically we go when it departs

The text prepares for the future, which entails its own death, which is not a tragic death. There's a bit of gallows humor to "we go" (we die) when "it departs" (it dies). A bit of ease, very different from "You must change your life," though change is precisely what's being verbalized.

Maybe it's because there's also continuity in change. Hejinian in "The Rejection of Closure": "the implication (correct) is that the words and the ideas (thoughts, perceptions, etc.—the materials) continue beyond the work."

BROKEN GLASS
earth dancing

… curious
[languages]

this is]
this is held

all around
yes, he says

it is the gender
that remembers

everything
everything

is apocalyptic
I know

I do not speak
for people[9]

---

[9] Cento composed of the ends of the following works (long poems or sequences which have been modified only lightly) in this order: Barbara Guest, "Türler Losses" (1979/1989); Ed Roberson, *Etai-Eken* (1975); George Oppen, "Of Being Numerous" (1968); Layli Long Soldier, "Whereas Statements" (2017); Myung Mi Kim, *Commons* (2002); Raúl Zurita, *Song for His Disappeared Love*, tr. Daniel Borzutzky (1985/2010); Brian Teare, "Doomstead Days" (2019); Etel Adnan, "Sea" (2012); C. D. Wright, *Deepstep Come Shining* (1998); and Tim Earley, *Linthead Stomp* (2016).

THE MOST ORDINARY of my days scans as an alternation between <reading> and <doing something other than reading>. Difficult to say when reading begins or ends. It's more like reading disperses into some other activity that bears the stain of reading. The gesture of lifting my head up at the end of a poem—it happens in a weather partly of the text I was reading and partly not.

Or, I'm always reading. Writing—that's reading too, only: practiced outwardly, for a public. In that practice I occasionally encounter a precision of language as well as a delight in that precision. Maybe that's all an epiphany is: a delight in the precision of language.

[END OF GISCOME ROAD]

We watched a gopher there[10]

---

10 Cento composed of the ends of: C. S. Giscombe, *Giscome Road* (1998) and Lorine Niedecker, "Lake Superior" (1968).

BECAUSE I teach writing I am often required to help "solve" the problem of a poem's ending. I no longer use textbooks and attempt to rely as little as possible on the anodyne, increasingly fixed bodies of craft knowledge that continue to get "passed" like DNA down the family trees of writing programs. But I too have my reflexes and when it comes to poem endings, I find I most often say (self-awareness™) something like

- *cut that last line? it's very loud;*
- *try moving the last line to the middle of the poem;*
- *the middle of the poem is the poem*[11] (yes, I realize these are variations on the same tune); or
- *write more!* (bit different, this one)

But workshop critique is the most minor aspect of teaching.

I think of teaching as a managed conversation of which I am the principal author (in perennial danger of becoming its authority). My authorial powers are spent in directing collective attention toward texts and practices I deem valuable; they disperse in discussion and are frequently thwarted by my students, to both my pleasure and my frustration.

Under this very general framework, so much can be done, so much can be re-routed. There's so much *I* want to do ... I threaten to become vague.

---

[11] I owe my teacher Carl Phillips for this one. I do pass on my own craft DNA; I just try to think on it before doing so.

Some specificities:

- In my classrooms, the greatest disruption to (or weapon against) the institution of US craft[12] has been teaching poetry in translation. Translation turns everything on its head, especially inveterate notions about originality and authorial intention.
- This semester (Spring 2020), I've been teaching a course on longform poetic composition. It is utterly liberating and we workshop nothing.
- I need to reconsider the terms of my poetics every time I speak them, especially when I teach.
- I mean to start talking about money more.
- I love love love teaching. I want to do it forever. I keep having to find honest and not unthinking ways to do so.

---

12 Caroline Levine: "Political scientists James March and Johan Olsen define institutions as 'relatively enduring collection[s] of rules and organized practices, embedded in structures of meaning and resources that are relatively invariant in the face of turnover of individuals and changing external circumstances.' Institutions endure, then, only because participants actively reproduce their rules and practices." It is in this sense I consider US craft an institution, which can be disrupted via an active derailing of its unexamined dogmas and disciplines.

TALK ABOUT MONEY MORE: It used to be I believed that bit by Robert Graves about there being "no money in poetry but … no poetry in money, either." There's definitely money in poetry, for some people; and maybe there's poetry in money also.

I don't know how to talk about money, just that I need to. I can acknowledge that I write, and teach writing, under/against/in accordance with the pressures of the university, the market, and social media, all of which have something to do with capital. I am a paid member of the US academe. I capitulate to capital on a daily basis. I make compromises in order to do the specific kinds of work I love to do (write, read, teach). But also: sometimes, often, I'm able to commit acts of antidiscipline[13] using precisely these works (writing, reading, teaching) that I love to do.

Thankfully, excellent research has begun to be done on the financial investments on and of US writing programs.[14] My own observations focus on what I'll call conceptual moneys of poetry:

- THE EPIPHANY AS MONEY SHOT. It's something like Wright's "I have wasted my life" but usually much worse. It acts as the salable essence of a poem. It's tweetable.

---

13 Michel de Certeau, tr. Steven Rendall: "innumerable practices by means of which users reappropriate the space organized by techniques of sociocultural production."

14 An abbreviated reading list: Eric Bennett's *Workshops of Empire*; Johannes Göransson's *Transgressive Circulation*; Mark McGurl's *The Program Era*. I am but beginning to track developments in this area.

It gets all the snaps in the event space. It's never brutal, but it can be tragic. It almost always follows the telling of an anecdote and is nostalgic. It's armchair psychology. It lacks mystery. My instincts tell me that the market seduces us into writing this way. It feels way too good—I don't trust it.

○ THE READER looms his grizzly head. It's taken me roughly a decade to realize that when someone in workshop (including a past-me) invokes The Reader, it is almost always for the purpose of staging an intervention in the unruly making of a text ("What's in it for The Reader?" one says, or, "This can be confusing for The Reader") while never having to admit, even to themselves, that The Reader *is* themself. I.e., if I were to point out to you that your poem is hard to read, I might say, "It's difficult for The Reader to follow," when what I really mean is, "It's difficult for *me* to follow." As psychological protection for the utterer, these kinds of phrasings are understandable enough. (Besides which, these formulae have been so long a part of our discourse, we likely pick them up simply because it appears that that is how an opinion *ought* to be expressed.) It seems safer, more polite, to say The Reader instead of "I"—but is it safer? I fear our repeated invocations of this phantom Reader have erected a very real presence at the outer edge of the classroom, awaiting our texts with His Most Discerning of Eyes. The Reader seems real, more real than the people in the room who are our actual readers. In the marketplace The Reader wields a strange baton whose movements we cannot understand but are given to follow. We pay ever closer attention to the median tune of the workshop and begin, perhaps, slowly to suss out The Reader's proclivities and desires. We've averaged out the instructions and now we think we know Him, and we can preach His Word to our own students. *Keep The Reader interested*, we say, *but not overwhelmed*. On the one hand, The Reader is our favorite boogeyman; on the other, He's the mean profile of a reading public whose desires appear to have been analyzed by a duly recompensed market research company. Let's kill The Reader.

○ PAY-OFFS. Something The Reader often wants is a *payoff* (a money shot). Poems also apparently have *stakes*. And a poem or poet can *earn* the right to do something that will not work if not *earned*. For example, one can *earn* the right to end a poem with something fuzzy like "I have wasted my life" by producing an appropriate amount of Imagism as an *advance* on that right. I have even heard that poets are required to demonstrate their craft bona fides in early publications if they wish, later, to engage in more experimental kinds of composition,[15] a sort of *quid pro quo* for wanting to break the rules. Once I begin to look, I discover more and more compensatory laws governing workshop aesthetics. What do they mean? What am I meant to do with them? I'm not interested in ridiculing particular individuals who engage in this kind of discourse (that would make me an extraordinary hypocrite) and certainly not anyone who considers themself to be a student. A rancor, however, is building in me. It is seeking its most explicit targets.

---

15 The opposition unwittingly set up between craft and experimentation is itself edifying—and amusing, and worth a whole other essay.

FOR A SOCIETY to move from the widespread use of coin money (metal objects of value, bearing inscriptions of value) to paper money (items of negligible value, bearing inscriptions of value) requires that society's ability to dissociate the symbol (the value of money) from its thing (the metal, the paper). The shift to electronic money[16] requires another round of quite profound evolutions in the collective reading of signs. These are the kinds of ideological transformations about meaning and matter that Marc Shell tracks in his book *Money, Language, and Thought* via close readings of key literary texts—like Poe's "The Gold Bug" and Shakespeare's *The Merchant of Venice*—and their sociohistorical contexts.

The book's greatest provocation is its incitement to attend the considerable extent to which we use money metaphors in our everyday language, in our literatures as well as discourses about literature. Language is full of money. We *coin* new words all the time; we hold people *accountable* for their actions; we *wager* our opinions. "A formal money of the mind," Shell argues, "informs all discourse and is as unaffected by whether or not the thematic content of a particular work includes money as by whether or not the material content of the ink in which the work may be inscribed includes gold." Which is to say, money thrives by means so pervasive and so internalized that all manner of transactions, including those that occur between authors and readers, or texts and readers, would seem to be *economic* ones.

---

[16] Shell: "The matter of electric money does not matter."

We can't rid ourselves of money metaphors any more than we can rid ourselves of money. But we can certainly attempt to lift the veil off these metaphors. Let's say we *owe* it to our work to do so. Shell: "thinking which fails to account for or even to encounter its own internalization of economic form remains insensitive to a sting that goads thought into becoming philosophy and, perhaps, into surpassing it."

KEEP THE READER INTERESTED ... BUT NOT OVER-WHELMED: Bizarrely, much of writing pedagogy is premised on ensuring The Reader *gets* something (whatever that is: epiphany, relatability, feelz, newness) out of a text while another chunk of it is geared toward attenuating *how much* The Reader gets. It's like Consumer Protection from too much Too Muchness in poetry. In my anecdotal experience, these are the sorts of things one might, for The Reader's sake, manage:

- sonic excess, wherein language approaches music or noise;
- multilingualism;
- arcane references, epigraphs, citations;
- word play, especially punning;
- emotion;
- abstraction;
- erudition, particularly in the form of "big words";
- and epiphany (the going rate is one per fourteen lines, from the All-Lyric-Poems-Are-Sonnets school of thought).

How to understand these anxieties over Too Muchness in poetry? Have they to do with The Reader being required to do *too much work* (deciphering) for *too little profit*? Or is it that The Poet is giving away too much *for free*?[17]

---

17 Imagine that the value of a paper note is its meaning and paper its form. If that paper note were glued to another paper note of equal value to create a single, thicker note—the gluing might be done neatly to produce an almost convincing, though heavier, note of the original kind; or it might be done clumsily, with bad glue and stubby fingers, creating a wrinkled

Maybe it has to do with the *use value* of technique. Many of my students allude to a principle they have already learned (or otherwise surmised from prevailing discourse) according to which a particular technique must be used for a particular purpose,[18] implying that an apparently purposeless use of artifice is a wasted opportunity.[19] Does it follow, then, that a technique having multiple purposes performs a different kind of wastefulness?

Injunctions against Too Muchness in poetry are, in other words, injunctions against pyrotechnics[20] or verbomania. They represent an anxiety over the money and meaning of form. A pyrotechnical poet can't be a lawful trader of crafts—they're a maniac upturning every polite system of exchange. Readers proliferate this mania via their own perversely productive kinds of reading. The regulated marketplace of meanings breaks down.

---

mess—does it now have more value (meaning) or less? If you were to make origami out of a paper note and spray it with a varnish that would make it rigid and unreturnable to its original form, what then? What is the state of the economy if there are too many paper notes circulating or too many counterfeit ones? What happens to meaning? Does it seem like the value of value is depreciating?

18 The notion of a purposeful technique recalls what Georges Bataille (tr. Allan Stoekl) says about "classical" or "material utility": its goal "is, theoretically, pleasure—but only in moderate form, since violent pleasure is seen as *pathological*."

19 But poetry *is* wasteful, says Bataille. It is a "nonproductive expenditure." It's perverse, irrational, profligate, and saturated with loss. Poetry "signifies ... creation by means of loss."

20 *Pyro* as in "fire." The arson that destroys—let's say, meaning.

In his book *Transgressive Circulation*, Johannes Göransson suggests that such anxieties over meaning derive from the reading model that was most influential in the development of US workshop pedagogies, New Criticism:

> I. A. Richards, the scholar who began the New Critical project which completely transformed the US practice of teaching and reading poetry, and which—as described by [Mark] McGurl in *The Program Era*—served as a major influence on the creation of the MFA workshop[,] based his aesthetics on a pedagogical model that focused on the communication of interiorities, or as [John Durham] Peters [in *Speaking into the Air*] puts it, the "accurate sharing of consciousness." What assures communication depends on readers having learned to read properly ("close reading"), which allows them to access the meaning of the poem, and to be "discriminating," thus able to determine the poem's "worth." In the end, the New Critical paradigm—like the communication ideal—functions according to an economic principle: meaning is a gold standard ensuring the value of language, while language is a currency otherwise susceptible to nonsense, inflation, chaos.

This is convincing—but I reckon also that anxieties about Too Muchness are terribly, deep-seatedly old. It's like a fear of people who speak in tongues or riddles, people too witty, too sly, to get a "straight" answer from. Shell locates the fear (or censure) of verbomania as far back as the medieval era whose theorists—following Aristotle's argument "that of all forms of generation usury is the most unnatural"— denounced "punning[,] its linguistic counterpart, since punning makes an unnatural, even a diabolical, supplement of meaning from a sound that is properly attached to only one (if any) meaning." As well, "'verbal usury' is an important technical term in the Jewish Talmud, in the Christian church fathers, and in the Islamic Traditions. There it refers to the generation of an illegal—the church fathers say unnatural—supplement to verbal meaning by "use of such methods as punning and flattering." Money, after all, wasn't invented yesterday.

AN "OTHER ECONOMY": Hejinian's "The Rejection of Closure" is an argument for the "open text" which does not provide closure, is open to readerly participation (i.e., making or *poesis*) and hermeneutic multiplicity, and "resists the cultural tendencies that seek to identify and fix material and turn it into a product; that is, it resists reduction and commodification." Hejinian finds that the "open text" engages in an alternative economy as described by Luce Irigaray: an economy that "diverts the linearity of a project, undermines the target-object of desire, explodes the polarization of desire on only one pleasure, and disconcerts fidelity to only one discourse."

ANOTHER "OTHER ECONOMY": Marc Shell defines the Holy Grail of medieval European tales as "an extraordinary gift both infinitely large and free, which was said to be able to lift men out of the ordinary world of exchange into a world in which freedom and totality were possible." The Grail is a gift that does not obligate its recipient. It exemplifies a wishful thinking deep-rooted in culture. Economically, it's a cornucopia—a gift that keeps on giving. The word "grail" itself is an etymological cornucopia.[21] Am I a renegade or a fossil for thinking poetry is a Grail? I can read it endlessly. Time is its money.

---

21 Shell: "there is in the grail tales a strictly linguistic economy, whose center is a marvelous word or its meaning. The word *grail* itself operates, in two complementary ways, as the center of this 'linguistic economy of abundance.' First, the sound of *graal*, associated with that of *kor*, is heard to give rise to such key terms as 'horn' (*cors*), 'body' (*cors*), 'court' (*cors*), 'heart' (*cuer*), and *Corbenic*. Clever etymology—or logic of verbal production—establishes the linguistic production of these words by pretending to work from them back to *graal*, their common primordial etymon. Second, the etymological process is reversed in such a way that the interpreter works from *graal* to older, historical etymons or contemporary cognates. Thus Hélinand says that *graal* comes from *gradatim*, because one puts food on it, as onto a dish; or from *gratus*, because it is pleasing to everyone. The grail, he explains, is a cornucopian dish that produces pleasing things. Similarly, Robert de Boron explains the grail as 'the platter that serves to satisfaction (*à gré*)' and calls it 'the grail that pleases [*agrée*].' The Didot *Perceval* makes the same etymological association: 'We call it *Graal* because it is so pleasing [*agrée*] to worthy men.' Finally *Merlin* calls the grail 'grace' itself: 'And these people call this vessel from which they have this grace [*grâsce*]—Grail [*Graal*].' ... [T]he word *graal* operates in the grail tales as a 'cornucopia of words.' just as the grail itself operates as a plentiful cornucopia of nourishing food."

LOVE—the preeminent litterateur (Amor,
Man in a Coma, Ma'am, Nemo, Amen)—speed
readers skim the white space of this galaxy,
its spoyld treee. Odd, the little wrigglings
and the chopped chirpings oddly rising
in perfect order: Taurus, Leo, Gemini rasping
their way round together and upward, tight
and seraphic. One rolled up hole roams in the
deep wave. All and no vessels are connected.
Now only time is wild, now fish the malevolent
tongue of night in its motionless veerition.[22]

---

22 Cento composed of the ends of: Mina Loy, *Songs to Joannes* (1917); Geoffrey Hill, *Speech! Speech!* (2000); Harryette Mullen, *S*PeRM**K*T* (1992); Jos Charles, *feeld* (2018); Gwendolyn Brooks, "In the Mecca" (1968); John Ashbery, "The Skaters" (1966); Roy Fisher, *A Furnace* (1986); Kim Hyesoon, "Manhole Humanity," tr. Don Mee Choi (2008/2011); Ursula Andkjær Olsen, *Third-Millennium Heart*, tr. Katrine Øgaard Jensen (2012/2017); Lisa Robertson, *Cinema of the Present* (2014); and Aimé Césaire, *Notebook of a Return to the Native Land*, tr. Clayton Eshleman and Annette Smith (1939/2001).

I'D LIKE to get back to where I began, with the ends of poems, by spending (hah!) a little time with that wickedest of pyromaniacs, Emily Dickinson. Her poem 280 tells of a "Funeral" happening in Dickinson's—*why bother with "the speaker"?*—"Brain." Its first four stanzas—

> I felt a Funeral, in my Brain,
> And Mourners to and fro
> Kept treading—treading—till it seemed
> That sense was breaking through—
>
> And when they were all seated,
> A service, like a Drum—
> Kept beating—beating—still I thought
> My Mind was going numb—
>
> And then I heard them lift a Box
> And creak across my Soul
> With those same Boots of Lead, again,
> Then Space—began to toll,
>
> As all the Heavens were a Bell,
> And Being, but an Ear,
> And I, and Silence, some strange Race
> Wrecked, solitary, here—

—are raucous with sound: the stomping about of mourners, the percussive nature of the service, the creaking of the floor under the leaden boots of pallbearers, and the "Bell" of the "Heavens." In the fifth and final stanza—

> And then a Plank in Reason, broke,

> And I dropped down, and down—
> And hit a World, at every plunge,
> And Finished knowing—then—

—the extended metaphor, as though by physics, breaks down when "a Plank in Reason" snaps and Dickinson falls through it, and herself, finally hitting—arriving at, figuring out, feeling—the world. It is at this point apparently that she "Finishe[s] knowing."

Seems straightforward enough, and linear in its telling—but as is generally the case with Dickinson, one might go on for pages discussing the fantastic wormholes of her syntax, the ambiguities of diction, and the way her tropes are sometimes nested inside other tropes[23] and … I'll just focus on the poem's illustration of how knowing happens and on how the poem ends.

---

23 For example, in the second stanza, the conceit of a funeral in the brain is elaborated via the description of "A service, like a Drum [that] Kept beating—beating." The service is part of the funeral trope. The drum is a simile for the funeral service: the collective sound of priest, choir, and congregation is, I suppose, like a beating drum. All this is happening inside the head. But the word "Drum" evokes also "Eardrum," which, anatomically, is located inside but near the edge of the head. A metaphorical and a literal drum are conflated, producing a preposterous, Mobius-strip-like, super sonically receptive membrane inside the cramped, figural space of the head. And later, in the fourth stanza, it even assumes a kind of exteriorized shape, a skin encasing the entire body or being (for here "Being" itself has become "but an Ear") painfully receiving an almost intolerable excess of sound.

I suppose I read the funeral in the brain as an epistemological struggle in which something has to die in order for knowing to happen. Also, this kind of knowing is the opposite of bodiless intellection. Everything is tangible. When I read, "it seemed / That Sense was breaking through," the idiomatic echo of "coming to one's senses" is a deception—for this is literally a body breaking apart under the severest conditions of sound.

In the final stanza, when the "Plank in Reason" breaks, that's the breakdown of a system and a selfhood. The brain itself is broken and subjectivity falls through its own body: knowing the world is a violent hitting against it in the dark. And it never stops ("at every plunge" is a peculiar phrase that seems to suggest falling is eternally renewed).

The poem-as-artifact does, however, stop. In the final line, "Finished knowing" could mean *I figured it out* or *I'm done with knowing because knowing is a failure*. Or it could mean *I'm dead* (etc.). I read "—then—" at least two ways: *at that moment I finished knowing* as well as *I finished knowing and after that [story redacted]*.

What comes after "—then—" can't be spoken because Dickinson (I) is (am) still falling through the cracks of the poem, hitting a world again and again.

THE EPIPHANY as Dickinson's "—then—."

What comes after "—then—" can't be *spoken*, but it can be *sensed* as a persistent residue of sound from all that thudding. Death is a noisy affair and thankfully so is poetry.

And so is, come to think of it, thinking. Lisa Robertson: "Listening or thinking moves in the thickness of what has been banished from identity: it moves in noise."

THE END of a poem as a middle. A fold between the text and the (redacted) future implied by the text.

Etel Adnan in *Journey to Mount Tamalpais*: "When you realize you are mortal you also realize the tremendousness of the future. You fall in love with a Time you will never perceive."

Me, in the prospectus for my dissertation, early 2016: "The future is the new Time Lost."

TIME LOST: Some current "ends" of mine.

Write more long poems.

Keep imagining Celan's "songs to be sung on the other side / of mankind."

Track Nathaniel Mackey's "Song of the Andoumboulou" and "mu" poems, which keep exceeding the ends of his books.

Keep thinking on Etel Adnan's "Time you will never perceive." And her "NIGHT" at the end of *The Arab Apocalypse*, after the death of the sun, the "NIGHT" in which "we shall find knowledge love and peace." Adnan as a poet not of epiphany but of revelation (or is one a category of the other?). Epiphany as a happening in the light; revelation a happening in the dark.

Keep thinking on the future[24] and its languages. Does future thinking mean thinking beyond one's death? Thom Donovan: "What Jalal Toufic calls 'undeath': undeath as a condition of possibility for remembrance, and for bearing witness to human and non-human (cosmic, terrestrial) cruelty." Jalal Toufic, in *Forthcoming*: "What is appropriate past the surpassing disaster is either a 'more sober, more factual ... "greyer"' language (Celan), or the dazzling colorful language of the messianics."

---

24 George Steiner: "Futurity is a necessary condition of ethical being."

Bibliography

Adnan, Etel. *The Arab Apocalypse*. Tr. Etel Adnan. The Post-Apollo Press, 2006.

Adnan, Etel. *Journey to Mount Tamalpais*. The Post-Apollo Press, 1986.

Adnan, Etel. *Of Cities & Women (Letters to Fawwaz)*. The Post-Apollo Press, 1993.

Adnan, Etel. "Sea." *Sea and Fog*. Nightboat Books, 2012.

Ashbery, John. "The Skaters." *Rivers and Mountains*. Ecco Press, 1977.

Bataille, Georges. "The Notion of Expenditure." *Visions of Excess: Selected Writings, 1927-1939*. Tr. Allan Stoekl. University of Minnesota Press, 1985.

Bennett, Eric. *Workshops of Empire: Stegner, Engle, and American Creative Writing during the Cold War*. University of Iowa Press, 2015.

Brooks, Gwendolyn. "In the Mecca." *Blacks*. Third World Press, 1987.

Celan, Paul. *Poems of Paul Celan: Revised and Expanded*. Tr. Michael Hamburger. Persea Books, 2002.

Césaire, Aimé. *Notebook of a Return to the Native Land*. Tr. Clayton Eshleman and Annette Smith. Wesleyan University Press, 2001.

Charles, Jos. *feeld*. Milkweed Editions, 2018.

De Certeau, Michel. *The Practice of Everyday Life*. Tr. Steven Rendall. University of California Press, 1984.

Deleuze, Gilles, and Félix Guattari. *A Thousand Plateaus: Capitalism and Schizophrenia*. Tr. Brian Massumi. University of Minnesota Press, 1987.

Dick, Maria-Daniella. "Epiphany." *The Edinburgh Dictionary of Modernism*. Eds. Vassiliki Kolocotroni and Olga Taxidou. Edinburgh University Press, 2018.

Dickinson, Emily. *The Complete Poems of Emily Dickinson*. Ed. Thomas H. Johnson. Little, Brown and Company, 1960.

Donovan, Thom. "Teaching Etel Adnan's *The Arab Apocalypse*." *Homage to Etel Adnan*. Eds. Lindsey Boldt, Steve Dickison, and Samantha Giles. The Post-Apollo Press, 2012.

Earley, Tim. *Linthead Stomp*. Horse Less Press, 2016.

"Epiphany." *The Christmas Encyclopedia*. Ed. William D. Crump. McFarland Books, 2013.

"Epiphany, n.2." *OED Online*. Oxford University Press, 2019.

Fisher, Roy. *A Furnace*. Flood Editions, 2018.

Giscombe, C. S. *Giscome Road*. Dalkey Archive Press, 1998.

Göransson, Johannes. *Transgressive Circulation: Essays on Translation*. Noemi Press, 2018.

Guest, Barbara. "Türler Losses." *Fair Realism*. Sun & Moon Press, 1989.

Hejinian, Lyn. *Happily*. The Post-Apollo Press, 2000.

Hejinian, Lyn. "The Rejection of Closure." *The Language of Inquiry*. University of California Press, 2000.

Hejinian, Lyn. "Some Notes Toward a Poetics." *American Women Poets in the 21st Century: Where Lyric Meets Language.* Eds. Claudia Rankine and Juliana Spahr. Wesleyan University Press, 2002.

Hill, Geoffrey. *Speech! Speech!.* Counterpoint, 2000.

Jabès, Edmond. *The Book of Questions: II & III.* Tr. Rosmarie Waldrop. Wesleyan University Press, 1976.

Kim, Hyesoon. "Manhole Humanity." *All the Garbage of the World, Unite!.* Tr. Don Mee Choi. Action Books, 2011.

Kim, Myung Mi. *Commons.* University of California Press, 2002.

Levine, Caroline. *Forms: Whole, Rhythm, Hierarchy, Network.* Princeton University Press, 2015.

Long Soldier, Layli. "Whereas Statements." *Whereas.* Graywolf Press, 2017.

Loy, Mina. "Songs to Joannes." *The Lost Lunar Baedeker: Collected Poems.* Farrar, Straus and Giroux, 1996.

McGurl, Mark. *The Program Era: Postwar Fiction and the Rise of Creative Writing.* Harvard University Press, 2009.

Mullen, Harryette. "S*PeRM**K*T." *Recyclopedia: Trimmings, S*PeRM**K*T, and Muse & Drudge.* Graywolf Press, 2006.

Niedecker, Lorine. "Lake Superior." *Lake Superior: Lorine Niedecker's Poem and Journal, Along with Other Sources, Documents, and Readings.* Wave Books, 2013.

Olsen, Ursula Andkjær. *Third-Millennium Heart.* Tr. Katrine Øgaard Jensen. Action Books, 2017.

Oppen, George. "Of Being Numerous." *New Collected Poems*. Ed. Michael Davidson. New Directions, 2002.

Rilke, Rainer Maria. *The Selected Poetry of Rainer Maria Rilke*. Ed. and tr. Stephen Mitchell. Vintage, 1982.

Roberson, Ed. *Etai-Eken*. University of Pittsburgh Press, 1975.

Robertson, Lisa. *Cinema of the Present*. Coach House Press, 2014.

Robertson, Lisa. *Nilling: Prose Essays on Noise, Pornography, the Codex, Melancholy, Lucretius, Folds, Cities and Related Aporias*. Book*hug, 2011.

Shell, Marc. *Money, Language, and Thought*. Johns Hopkins University Press, 1993.

Steiner, George. *After Babel: Aspects of Language and Translation*. 3rd ed. Oxford University Press, 1998.

Teare, Brian. "Doomstead Days." *Doomstead Days*. Nightboat Books, 2019.

Wright, C. D.. *Deepstep Come Shining*. Copper Canyon Press, 1998.

Wright, James. *The Branch Will Not Break*. Wesleyan University Press, 1963.

Zucker, Rachel. "An Anatomy of the Long Poem." *Poets.org*, https://poets.org/text/anatomy-long-poem.

Zurita, Raúl. *Song for His Disappeared Love*. Tr. Daniel Borzutzky. Action Books, 2010.

The End
© Aditi Machado, 2020

2020 Pamphlet Series
ISBN 978-1-946433-44-2
First Edition, First Printing
Edition of 1,000

Ugly Duckling Presse
The Old American Can Factory
232 Third Street, #E-303
Brooklyn, NY 11215
uglyducklingpresse.org

Distributed in the USA by SPD/Small Press Distribution
Distributed in the UK by Inpress Books

Series design by chuck kuan and Sarah Lawson
Typeset by Don't Look Now!
Type is New Century Schoolbook
Cover paper and flyleaf from French Paper Co.
Printed offset and bound at McNaughton & Gunn
Flyleaf printed letterpress at Ugly Duckling Presse

This publication is made possible, in part, by support from the New York State Council on the Arts, a state agency. This project is supported by the Robert Rauschenberg Foundation.

 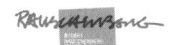

This pamphlet is part of UDP's 2020 Pamphlet Series: twenty commissioned essays on poetics, translation, performance, collective work, pedagogy, and small press publishing. The authors are listed below; their pamphlets are available for individual purchase and as a subscription (uglyducklingpresse.org/subscribe). Each offers a different approach to the pamphlet as a form of working in the present, an engagement at once sustained and ephemeral.

Mirene Arsanios
Omar Berrada
Sergio Chejfec
Don Mee Choi
Kunci Study Forum & Collective
Iris Cushing
Simon Cutts
Nicole Cecilia Delgado
Adjua Gargi Nzinga Greaves
Dimitra Ioannou

Sibyl Kempson
Claudia La Rocco
Aditi Machado
Chantal Maillard
Tinashe Mushakavanhu
Sawako Nakayasu
Tammy Nguyen
Aleksandr Skidan
Steven Zultanski
Magdalena Zurawski

To win a subscription, write to office@uglyducklingpresse.org with your solution to the following puzzle: Using only 6 straight lines, divide the circle on the back cover so that each number is in its own section, without any overlap between numbers.